R.A.I.D.

The Cognitive Reframing Mindset Strategy

By: Ariel Yosef

Table of Contents

Defining R.A.I.D.

To put it simply, this four-step mindset reframing strategy will help you to not only be more efficient, but hardwire your brain into processing adversity in a more sustainable way. You will be able to identify solutions to challenges that have previously seemed overwhelming, eliminate overthinking, as well as restructure the way you take in information.

The R.A.I.D. mindset has not only helped me in my life, but has helped everyone close to me, like my friends, family, and even my colleagues. This strategy is a tool for people to become the best version of themselves in any aspect of their life. Whether it is romantic relationships, money, self-development, or something a little more spiritual,

R.A.I.D. helps you assess and make a decision based on the relevant information present to you.

Although this may sound like an easy task, reframing your cognitive processes will be like any other worthwhile goal you partake in life. It will require training your brain and building up those muscles that allow you to instantly and instinctively think and decide in a way that is solution focused. For example, somebody who has never exercised in their life decides to go to the gym for the first time. They will have a much harder time lifting weights, or exercising, compared to someone who has done so for years. The secret to being and becoming successful in this area, or any area at all, is to just show up. Sooner or later, referring back to the example, the individual who had trouble working out in the beginning will begin to improve in their performance month by month and year by year. The only thing that this person has to do is make a decision to be consistent and commit to their goal. After that, nature does the rest and they will slowly become a manifestation of themselves that has been conceptualized over the span of their lifetime. In that regard, everyone has an image of who they are and where they want to be, which is a healthy thing to carry with you while pursuing your goals, it may even be someone's "reason why", however before I digress, let's talk about what R.A.I.D. means.

R.A.I.D. Is the process of relinquishing, assessing, internalizing, and deciding. Now this may not make sense right away, but as I explain further, each step will become more and more clear.

Relinquish

First of all, what does relinquish mean and how is it applied here? For starters, to relinquish something is to, "voluntarily cease to keep or claim; give up". There is a lot of meaning behind this definition and here's why. By relinquishing something–the negative thoughts, the paranoia, the black and white thinking, or the anxiety of a situation–you are choosing, voluntarily, to let go and abandon that particular thing. See most people have gotten into the bad habit of abandoning their dreams or goals, yet the easiest and most reasonable thing they need to abandon, for the sake of achieving their goals and dreams, is the toxic thinking that prevents them from getting there. Taking the first step of any process is the hardest, and in general, the first step in the R.A.I.D. mindset strategy is the most difficult. The reason why relinquishing is the hardest and equally most important step, is because self-regulating is one of the most difficult things to do on this planet, however by mastering this step, you will be able to master it all with ease. The reason why it is difficult to self-regulate is because a person dealing with a stressful ultimatum, or someone dealing with anxiety because of an unpredictable circumstance, will not realize that they are preventing their mind from making sound and valid decisions. The fight or flight mechanism in our bodies is what is being activated during these times, and it will affect everyone differently. During this mode, or rather process; adrenaline is being released into our body and it is like we have been transported to the base of a mountain millennia ago, where we have to decide to fight or run from a wild animal. To gain control over your mind during a time of heightened brain activity, an individual will have to remain calm. Of course this may be easier said than done, but this step is crucial for R.A.I.D. to be sustainable. Regaining rhythmic breathing by taking a deep breath, or two, might be necessary in highly impactful situations. Being calm will allow you to think clearly and create an internal environment where you are able to pinpoint those negative thoughts and willingly abandon them.

*The following are a couple of vignettes that will address this process.

1.)

"A young adult male and a young adult female are sexually active. They have been sexually active throughout their relationship and have never had a pregnancy scare. In addition, they are both graduating college and starting careers in their respective fields. Moreover, as time went on, the young female adult was feeling symptoms that match the criteria for pregnancy, so just to make sure and put her mind at ease, she decided to take a test. To her surprise, the pregnancy test said she was pregnant! She could not believe what she saw and took multiple, however the results were all the same. Not knowing whether to feel happy, sad, or worried, she tells her boyfriend in a panic. During this extremely difficult scenario, they both feel desperate for an answer or a way out."

Response: For this couple to make the best decision for themselves, they will have to relinquish stigma regarding keeping the baby or abortion from a biopsychosocial standpoint. What this means is that for them to objectively look at their lives and make a decision with the least amount of influence as possible, they must abandon and let go of certain fears, anxieties, and stigma from a biological, psychological, and social standpoint. Although there are certain things that may be difficult to fight against, like our genetics and brain chemistry, we still have the power to shift and guide our decisions by reframing our thoughts, which will ultimately lead to the best possible outcome.

How would you react using the Relinquish step in R.A.I.D.?

_____

_____

_____

_____

_____

_____

_____

_____

_____

2.)

"An individual decides that they are tired of living paycheck to paycheck and are ready to start finding a way to break that cycle. They begin to watch a lot of youtubers promote different kinds of wealth building strategies, however they find that they are not passionate about any of them. After hours of searching for different ways of shifting their reality, they still feel as though they are no closer than when they first started. They end up not choosing a path or direction because they fear failure, worry about what their social group might think, and because they plainly feel overwhelmed. As a result, they feel as though they have lost time, sleep and energy.

Response: This vignette expresses the desire of an individual who wants to change or alter their financial reality. For them to succeed in their journey, they must be able to take a step back and begin with the root of the problem. The root of their problem happens to be an underlying fear of failure, rejection, and information. To elaborate, this individual will need to abandon the concept of failure or rejection by reframing what it actually means. The assessment and internalization portion of R.A.I.D. will speak more in depth on behalf of this, however for the purpose of this vignette, the individual has to first remove their previous way of thinking. It would not be called growth if it did not take some effort or pain–hence the phrase, "growing pains". So for them to succeed in finding their direction, they must give up on their outdated mindset and begin reinforcing the thoughts that will get them to where they want to be–planting the seed.

What would you tell this individual after mastering the Relinquish portion of R.A.I.D.?

_____

_____

_____

_____

_____

_____

_____

_____

_____

_____

_____

_____

Assess

After you shed the toxic waste that has been plaguing your mind, long-term or short-term, it is now time to assess the situation at hand, or the thing that has been a significant confrontation for you. During this step of R.A.I.D. you will be analyzing the situation to the best of your ability and asking yourself questions. This step is extremely important to implement and will allow you to put everything you need into perspective. For this to work effectively, you will have to ask yourself yes or no questions that pertain to the challenge at hand. By answering these questions, this method will allow you to see what to actually prioritize. Go ahead and give it a try! Think of something that has been bugging you lately and cycle through the questions.

These questions follow a general format, although I strongly recommend asking questions that pertain specifically to the obstacle.

General Yes or No Questions that can Apply:

- Is this really the issue?

- Am I wasting my time worrying?

- Am I lying to myself?

- Am I allowing my negative thoughts to prevail?

- Do I possess all of the skills I need to conquer this on my own?

- Is there something else I am not seeing?

- Am I overreacting?

- Do I need to work harder?

- Do I need to be more patient?

- Is there a solution?

- Am I letting external factors dictate what I do and where I go?

- Do I have a support system?

*Note–these are general questions that you do not need to use. You may make up your own that are more specific to the obstacle you are facing. Make these questions yes or no questions that pertain to the obstacle at hand. Use the example below for a reference.

Here is a real example that has applied to my life, you may find this to be a helpful guide when applying your own assessment. For this example, I will reflect on past experiences.

Example:

I am a recent college graduate who wants to start working and earn my place in the world. The obstacle in front of me is figuring out what I can use my degree for. Should I stay within the parameters of a system I have been taught to be a part of, or should I take a risk and start my first business? I am apprehensive of the latter, however I do not shy away from challenges. I know that this will be a financial burden in the beginning, although there is hope for a better future. Knowing my academic past, I can easily find a job that will suffice if I were an average person—I am not.

For this example specifically, I had asked myself these questions:

- Am I scared to try? (you will never know if you don't try.)

- Is there a way I can do both (start my business and work?)

- Is it in my control to determine the outcome of my future?

- Do I have a support system? (Find one—people who will help lift you up.)

- Can I rely on myself to commit?

- Is this an obstacle that has to do with my mindset?

- Can I identify opportunity?

Reflection:

By answering truthfully to all of these questions, I was able to determine the things that I was in control of that could alter the course of my life. For example, I was scared, however fear meant that I was headed in the right direction. Furthermore, by being able to answer yes to all of the questions above, I gained confidence to continue down the path that I felt was the most successful and pursuable at the time. I ultimately made the decision to work and build my business on the side until I felt a shift was necessary. This for me, and hopefully for you, in whatever area of life you are facing an obstacle in, can lead to laying down the first brick towards building the life you desire.

It Is important to understand that if the issue resides within the mindset of an individual, then that is the obstacle they must focus on during their implementation of R.A.I.D. Additionally, they will be able to ultimately shift their mindset and reuse R.A.I.D. to cycle the next obstacle or challenge. Towards the end of the next step, or rather; process, this particular individual and others facing different obstacles, will finally be able to start seeing the light at the end of the tunnel by enacting the process of internalization.

Internalization

Moving onward, the definition that applies best to the process of internalization regarding R.A.I.D. is as follows: "The process of internalization begins with learning what the norms are. The individual will undergo a process of understanding why they are of value, until they finally accept the norm as their own viewpoint.". To understand if something is of value—an idea, resource, or mindset, you will have to look at the prospect under realistic terms and think creatively about what it can do for you.

After relinquishing your negative thoughts and assessing the obstacle in front of you, in an easy and concise way, you will enter into the internalization phase with a deeper understanding of the direction and norms that need to change. This step is vital in reframing your mindset because it will allow you to begin defoliating the unnecessary norms you have adopted up until this point. It is essential and crucial to be able to identify what those norms are and begin removing them from the repertoire of your identity.

Now that you have gone through the first two steps of this process, you are able to rationally isolate and locate the norms that may be interfering with your growth. This mindset strategy is not for the faint hearted because it will require you to be honest and authentic with yourself. From then on, you will be planting new seeds which you will water daily until they can stand on their own. In addition, figuring out what norms have been plaguing your growth as an individual will require you to ask yourself some open ended questions. This has to relate to the goal or obstacle you have identified in the beginning of this process. Use this time to reflect on past experiences to find any similarities with your behavior. By doing this, it will allow you to correctly recognize the inhibitors in your life. Moreover, some obstacles will require more thought than others, however it is not an excuse for stagnation. By keeping the momentum you have been building up throughout this cognitive reframing process, you will be able to reach the final step of R.A.I.D. where you will decide on a plan and commit to it. Removing your current perception from the norm, or removing a norm that is hindering your growth, is vital for the success of implanting the new one.

After you have finally decided on the norms that need to be altered or removed, begin to conceptualize and administer love and care as if you were raising a child. For example, if the old norm was that you, as a woman, don't play sports well, or that because you have a disability, mental or physical, you cannot live a happy life, or make money, then the new norms would directly contrast that. Every single time there is an opportunity to restructure and reframe, use the process of internalization by means of positive self-talk. "Women CAN play sports and they CAN play them well—even better than men!. I have a disability, but I CAN still succeed, I CAN live a happy life, and I CAN make money. Believing in your yourself and in the process is one of the most significant acts of growth that you can commit to. Most people are embarrassed or feel guilty because it feels like starting all over again, however compared to the amount of people that do not even take the first step, you are already ahead of the game. Movement, energy, and momentum only take one primary mover to set things into an infinite motion. Why can't this be you? There is nothing to fear. Time is limited—make the most out of it by doing the things that make you happy to be alive on this Earth. Remind yourself daily that it IS POSSIBLE to do what you have set your mind to and that YOU WILL do it. This is how internalization, using R.A.I.D., supports the growth of new norms that you have chosen to set for yourself.

*Note—Norms can be societal or cultural factors that can vary between regions. Norms represented in the above paragraph are used for instructional purposes and as a general reflection of current stigma.

Decide

You have now crossed over to the final step of the R.A.I.D. cognitive reframing process. By doing so, you will now have to develop a realistic plan of action beginning now. Throughout this process, you have relinquished everything negative and useless, assessed your own predisposition regarding mindset, and internalized new norms in the face of the obstacle at hand. The final step is to ACT! Standing idly by is not an option anymore, you have reached the culmination of shifting your mindset, so there is only one thing left to do. In this chapter, we will focus on the steps we need to take in order for our mindset to flourish in the reflection of our behavior, not just in one situation, but in all situations. BE DECISIVE.

For starters, focus on one thing that will allow you to make the leap and take the first step towards acting upon your newfound mindset. This step should be realistic, achievable, and receive your full commitment. Show up for yourself in this way so that you can apply this framework to guide the successes along your path to fulfillment. This process will be as effective as what you put into it, so to start creating the habit of decisiveness, you will need to build upon small achievable tasks that will ultimately, and eventually, compound on themselves—allowing you to gain the confidence you need for R.A.I.D to be sustainable for the rest of your life.

By making it this far into the R.A.I.D. reframing process, you have already altered the internal environment that has been hindering your growth. The main focus now, is to NOT act upon the wants you might have, but ACT on the needs that will support you, residually, throughout this journey. These small achievable tasks can be anything that fit into the parameters of what is considered attainable for the individual. You have already begun to be honest and authentic with yourself, so finding out what these tasks are will be easy. Your tasks can range anywhere from taking a walk, drinking an extra bottle of water a day, enrolling in class, signing up for groups, getting a job, starting a business, or consulting with someone. Make the conscious decision to commit to this task, and future tasks, and watch how you will slowly develop an instinct towards successfully dealing with struggle.

Finally, you will have cemented rational and quick decision-making into your life forever. You will be able to use these fundamental skills in order to successfully respond to the obstacles that you will inevitably face in your lifetime. When in doubt, refer to this process again and use the skills you have already built to relinquish, assess, internalize, and decide once more.

Motivating Quotes

"Your house is only as strong as your foundation."

"Be the change that you want to see in the world."

"Focus on the what, not on the if."

"One small act can also be one giant leap!"

"The longevity of happiness is found in the pursuit of something."

"If you never try you will never know."

"We need to accept that we won't always make the right decisions, that we'll screw up royally sometimes—understanding that failure is not the opposite of success, it's part of success." –Arianna Huffington

"It's how you get hit and keep moving forward."

"You've gotta dance like there's nobody watching, love like you'll never be hurt, sing like there's nobody listening, and live like it's heaven on earth." –William W. Purkey

"When one door of happiness closes, another opens; but often we look so long at the closed door that we do not see the one which has been opened for us." –Helen Keller

"Do one thing every day that scares you."— Eleanor Roosevelt

"Happiness is not something ready-made. It comes from your own actions."—Dalai Lama XIV

"If you believe something will happen then it will."

"Impossible is just an opinion"—Paulo Coelho

"Hold the vision, trust the process."

"One day, or day one—you decide."

"Invest in the version of the person you will become."

"We are what we repeatedly do. Excellence, then, is not an act, but a habit." –Aristotle

"The hard days are what make you stronger."

"If the opportunity doesn't knock, build a door."

"Hard work beats talent."

"Work hard for what you want because it won't come to you without a fight. You have to be strong and courageous and know that you can do anything you put your mind to. If somebody puts you down or criticizes you, just keep on believing in yourself and turn it into something positive."—Leah LaBelle

"Everyone has inside them a piece of good news. The good news is you don't know how great you can be! How much you can love! What you can accomplish! And what your potential is."

–Anne Frank

"Be who you are meant to be!"

–Ariel Yosef

www.ingramcontent.com/pod-product-compliance
Lightning Source LLC
Chambersburg PA
CBHW070349300526
45791CB00023B/1520